Taking Care of Me

So I Can Take Care of My Children

by Barbara Carlson, Margaret Healy, and Glo Wellman

Illustrated by Margaret Healy

Tools for Everyday Parenting Series

Parenting Press, Inc.
Seattle, Washington

First edition
Printed in the United States of America

ISBN 1-884734-02-2 Paperback
ISBN 1-884734-03-0 Library binding

Cover and text design by Cameron Mason
Cover illustration by Karen Pew

Library of Congress Cataloging-in-Publication Data
Carlson, Barbara, 1948–
    Taking care of me (so I can take care of my children) / Barbara Carlson, Margaret Healy, Glo Wellman ;
illustrated by Margaret Healy. -- 1st ed.
        p.   cm. -- (Tools for everyday parenting series)
    Includes index.
    ISBN 1-884734-03-0 (library). -- ISBN 1-884734-02-2 (paper)
    I. Parenting--Psychological aspects.   2. Parents--Psychology.   3. Self-realization.   4. Teenage parents--
of me.   V. Series.
Life skills guides.   I. Healy, Margaret, 1941–   .   II. Wellman, Glo, 1950–   .   III. title.   IV. Title: Taking care
HQ755.8.C375   1998
649'.1--dc20

                                                94-23012
                                                CIP

Parenting Press, Inc.
P.O. Box 75267
Seattle, Washington 98175
www.ParentingPress.com

Contents

Parenting is easier when you feel good.

About This Book

Taking Care of Me (So I Can Take Care of My Children) is a little book about a big part of being a good parent.

Have you noticed how much easier life is when you feel good? The day seems to go more smoothly. There aren't so many hassles. The kids get along better. What you need to do gets done. Everyone around you is more cooperative.

In contrast, when you feel bad, the feeling seems to rub off on everyone and everything. The baby cries constantly. The chores take forever. The older kids can't do anything right. The car won't run. In short, life is a pain.

How parents are feeling affects their children. The better you feel, the better your children will feel. *Taking Care of Me* is full of ideas and tools to help you take charge of how you feel and what you do. Our goal is to help you make the most of every day with your family.

Parents who take care of *themselves* take better care of their children. To take good care of yourself, it helps to—

- Understand and accept yourself
- Be aware of feelings and thoughts
- Take time to have fun and renew energy
- Handle stresses so they don't get you down
- Have confidence that you can do a good job
- Give love and accept love

Parenthood takes a great deal of work. Every day you get up planning to do the best job you can. When things don't go well one day, you try again the next day. Learning how to take care of yourself will make your job as a parent easier.

Part One

Getting to Know Myself

People are made up of many unique characteristics.

Look Inside

Every person has many unique characteristics. Like puzzle pieces, these characteristics fit together to make a whole person.

As distinct individuals, everyone has the following—

- Temperament (personality)
- Body (physical traits)
- Basic needs
- Feelings and behavior
- Natural abilities

These characteristics are present at birth. They are a part of who you are today. They influence how your parents raised you and how you guide your children.

Unique temperaments are present at birth.

LISA, PLEASE STOP PUSHING. LEARN TO WAIT YOUR TURN!

EVEN AS A LITTLE GIRL I FELT I HAD TO GET ATTENTION BY BEING AGGRESSIVE.

. . .

I'M GLAD I KNOW HOW TO USE THAT ENERGY POSITIVELY NOW.

THANK YOU, HONEY, BUT DARRIN IS SO SHY. HE'LL GET TO KNOW YOU AFTER A WHILE.

SINCE MY CHILDHOOD I'VE HAD TROUBLE ADJUSTING TO NEW PLACES AND PEOPLE.

. . .

I MAKE AN EXTRA EFFORT NOW.

Your temperament. Each person is born with a unique temperament, made up of various traits. You may have noticed this about your friends. One may be very social and seem to know everything about everybody. Another may rush through life, playing and working hard. A third may spend much time thinking and figuring out things. Temperaments are neither good nor bad; they just are—like eye color or skin tone, for example.

Each temperament trait is useful sometimes and not so helpful at other times. A good listener may not like to give speeches or lead meetings, for example. An active person may feel very frustrated with a bookkeeper's job. Understanding your temperament helps you be a better parent. You will understand why you react to your children as you do.

There are nine temperament traits. Some people are high in one or two areas. Many people are in the "middle of the road" in others. Check the areas in which your temperament is strong. Once you have figured out your temperament, do the same for your partner and your children.

Nine temperament traits

Activity level
High activity and
energy levels

| | | | | | | Low energy and rarely fidgety |

Intensity
Intense whether they
are happy or mad

| | | | | | | Quiet and reserved most of the time |

Approach/withdrawal
Easily approach
new people or situations

| | | | | | | Resists most new things at first |

Adaptability
Adapt quickly to change
regardless of their initial opinion

| | | | | | | Take weeks or months to adapt |

Sensitivity to physical world
Extremely aware of light, sound, temperature, and texture of clothes, etc.

Totally unaware of the physical world

Persistence
Stay with a task for a long time, even for things they have difficulty with

Move from one activity to another frequently

Regularity
Have a precise internal clock. Eat, sleep, and toilet at the same time each day

Have an irregular clock. May sleep six hours one night and 12 the next

Mood
Born happy, cheerful, and optimistic

Often irritable and upset

Distractibility
Easily distracted by activities going on around them

Unaware of or rarely distracted by people, noise, or activity

13

Children's temperaments. Understanding *your child's temperament* also helps you be a more effective parent. When you have a child who is very different from you, parenting can be challenging. Your own parents may have had a hard time raising you if your temperament was different from theirs.

Understanding temperaments helps you accept yourself and your children. It also helps you have reasonable expectations for yourself and others. Parents and children *can learn* acceptable behavior and useful skills. This is possible no matter how challenging their temperaments are. Keep in mind that all traits are useful in some situations and not so in others.

Exercise helps you cope with stress.

Your body. Like temperaments, bodies are neither good nor bad. They just are. We often feel we need to change our bodies. We want to be thinner or plumper; shorter or taller; and so on. The only aspect we can control to a large degree is our health. Nearly everyone has a physical challenge or two by adulthood. The important thing is to learn how to manage as well as possible.

To help your body—

- Eat nutritious foods that help restore and maintain health.
- Get enough rest so that you can cope with life.
- Exercise your body and your mind to maintain physical and mental flexibility.
- Get medical attention when you need it.
- Do activities that are fun for you. Everyone needs to have fun.

By taking care of yourself you are setting an example that your children can follow.

Basic needs must be met for good health.

Your basic needs. Everyone has basic needs. We all need to feel good physically and emotionally.

Physical needs
Food
Sleep
Health care
Safe place to live

Emotional needs
Love and acceptance by others
Control in our lives
Fair and respectful treatment
Chance to learn and practice skills

Some people have special needs. Among these are physical and mental disabilities, an inability to work, and illness. People with special challenges may need more help from family, friends, and community. Perhaps you have such needs, or you know someone who does.

Unmet needs show up in our behavior.

Unmet needs. If our basic physical and emotional needs are not satisfied, we can't be the best parents we could be. Parents with babies who wake and cry during the night know how hard it is to be patient. Their need for sleep is not being met. Anyone who doesn't have a safe place to live will likely have trouble keeping a job. Worry and fatigue may prevent them from doing good work.

Sometimes unmet needs from childhood affect how we feel and how we behave toward our children. Temperament traits plus unmet needs act together to influence our parenting. For example, a reserved person who didn't get enough attention as a child may not know how to give her children the attention they need.

How we feel often affects how we behave.

I GUESS CAROL
ISN'T COMING.
I'M UPSET!
I HAVE BEEN COUNTING ON
THIS TIME TOGETHER!!

I THINK I DID IT!
THIS LOOKS AS GOOD
AS NEW!

JOEY, STOP WHINING! I CAN'T
READ TO YOU TONIGHT. I
HAVE A HEADACHE!

HONEY, I FIXED IT! LET'S
TRY IT OUT
TOGETHER

Feelings and behavior. How we feel often affects how we behave. Sometimes feelings affect behavior very strongly. We do things which make us feel proud. Some things we do we regret very deeply.

How we feel about ourselves on the inside shows on the outside. Other adults, and children especially, react to how we feel. Have you ever noticed how your children are hard to manage when you're tired or worried? When you feel good about yourself, however, your children tend to behave better.

When we feel frustrated we may blame others for our circumstances. Blaming can be a tempting way to deal with stress. It's easy to say, "I can't help the way I am. My parents fought all the time." Or, "I don't have to put up with this. It's all my boss's fault. I'll quit this job."

In Part Two of this book you will learn better ways to handle stress.

Your natural abilities can lead to fulfilling life work.

Natural abilites. Everyone is unique in their natural abilities or talents. Have you ever thought, "My friend is so talented. She can make everything around her look pretty." What we do well often comes easily to us. People like to do what they do best and most easily. Those who have no chance to do what they do best are sometimes unhappy.

It is easiest to gain added skill in areas in which you have some talent. Often you can tell what people's natural talents are by observing what they do to make a living.

Make a list of things you like to do best. You will be happiest with fun and work in which you use your natural abilities.

Influences from the Outside

In the last chapter we talked about the characteristics people are born with. Now we will talk about the family influences and life experiences that also make up who you are.

Life experiences include—

- Experiences growing up
- Relationships with others
- Learned skills
- Values
- Goals

Situations, events, and people around us add to the mix of who we are. How we grew up influences how we respond to life's events today.

How you grew up influences your life today.

ALONSO, DO YOU EVER MISS THE FAMILY AND RELIGIOUS CELEBRATIONS FROM OUR PAST?

THE ENTIRE NEIGHBORHOOD WOULD GET TOGETHER! I THINK I MISS THE MUSIC, THE ACTIVITIES, AND THE SHARING.

WHAT IF WE CELEBRATED MARIA'S BIRTHDAY WITH OUR NEIGHBORS. WE COULD BEGIN AT CHURCH, AND THEN HAVE OUR FESTIVITIES IN THE PARK.

YOU AND YOUR FRIENDS CAN PROVIDE MUSIC. OUR RELATIVES AND I CAN PREPARE FOODS FROM OUR CULTURE...

THE CHILDREN CAN HELP MAKE PIÑATAS AND DECORATE.

MARIA'S BIRTHDAY

MIRANDA, THIS HAS BEEN SO WONDERFUL!

Experiences growing up. We all grew up in different circumstances. Some of these different circumstances are found in—

- Family and friends
- Neighborhood we grew up in
- Schools we attended and teachers we had
- Religious background
- Native language and ethnic culture

Whether our homes were financially stable or not, happy or not, healthy or not, affects how we get along in the world today. Everyone has had a combination of good and bad experiences. That is the way life is. We don't have total control over our lives. We can, however, decide how to *respond* to life's events, good and bad.

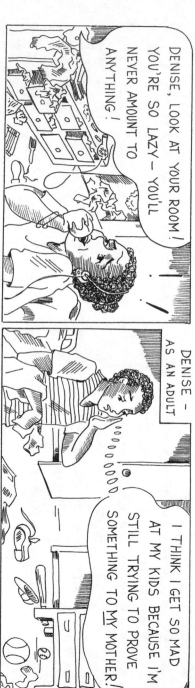

Relationships with others. No one picks parents, siblings, children, grand-parents, aunts and uncles. . . . But all of these family members contributed to who you are and they still influence you today.

We do pick our own friends and partners. Some relationships may be healthy and others harmful. Your experiences with the people in your life play a part in who you are today.

Whether we choose our relationships or inherit them, all people have an affect on us. Have you ever noticed yourself saying, "I sound just like my mother." Or, "I yell at the kids the way my father yelled at me when I was growing up." Understanding past and present relationships may help you get along better with your children and partner.

Skills. As we grow up, we learn how to do many things. Different people know different things because of the different circumstances they have grown up in. We all know some of the same things. What you learned growing up and as an adult is a part of you now. All of us feel confident in some areas and less so in others. If you want to learn how to do more things, you can.

Many of us feel we can't do certain things because we didn't get support as children. Maybe someone made fun of us. Maybe we compared ourselves to a brother or sister, and then got discouraged. Parents don't always realize that children need lots of encouragement as they learn new skills.

✔ ACTIVITY: What do you know how to do?

- ☐ Parenting
- ☐ Cooking
- ☐ Sports
- ☐ Reading
- ☐ Math
- ☐ Fixing cars
- ☐ Teaching
- ☐ Woodworking
- ☐ Cleaning
- ☐ Farming

- ☐ Drawing
- ☐ Sewing
- ☐ Leading others
- ☐ Music
- ☐ Communicating
- ☐ Building
- ☐ Gardening
- ☐ Plumbing
- ☐ Writing
- ☐ Entertaining

- ☐ Solving problems
- ☐ Caring for animals
- ☐ Playing with kids
- ☐ Acting in plays
- ☐ Using a computer
- ☐ Driving a car
- ☐ Listening well
- ☐ Organizing things
- ☐ Helping people
- ☐ Making things

You can see from this list that you have learned how to do many things. What else would you like to learn? What are three steps you can take to start learning what you want to know?

Your values. Values are the ideas and beliefs we live by. They are different for everyone. Some values that many people hold in common are—

- Taking care of themselves and their families
- Treating others kindly and respectfully
- Following the laws of the community

Make a list of the values you live by. Do you want your children to live by them, too?

Your goals. Goals are the things we work toward. These vary from person to person. Some people have the goal to be caring parents. Some people want to learn a trade that allows them to earn a living by doing physical work. Others want to go to college. Having a goal can help you achieve something important to you. It can give meaning to your life and to the work you choose. Most goals are based on things or qualities that you value.

✔ ACTIVITY: Set a goal for yourself

Goal setting is important. You can change your life by learning and practicing this skill.

1. *Decide what you would like to do.* Be specific about the activity or behavior.
2. *Make a list of all the steps you need to take to reach your goal.* Write them down or talk about them. Then you'll be able to check off items as you do them.
3. *Decide when you will do each step.* How often? How long?
4. Figure out what reward you would like to give yourself when you have reached your goal. It could be as simple as taking half an hour to enjoy a cup of coffee or tea. It may be as complicated as getting a babysitter and going to a movie. You deserve something for reaching your goal!

When you feel good you can do more.

Understanding Feelings

Children and adults—all people—are happiest when they feel good about themselves. This good feeling is *self-esteem*. When we feel good, we can use our energy to do all sorts of things. We can even make positive changes in our lives.

People with high self-esteem feel as if they're in charge. They have the power to meet life's challenges. They take risks because they know they are still okay even if they make a mistake. To change things means taking risks. What you try first may not work. You will need to keep trying.

How do you get self-esteem, that good feeling that makes change possible?

Uncomfortable feelings tell you to change something.

Start by noticing all your feelings. When you feel good, it is usually easy to understand why you feel that way. Someone was thoughtful. You finished a task you had set out to do. You felt love for your children.

At other times it's hard to understand what you're feeling. Words and actions don't always go together. You may tell someone "I'm fine" when you're really *not*. Maybe you are feeling nervous or upset. You may not know why you feel this way, but you find yourself taking it out on others, including your children.

It is important to recognize all of your feelings. *Uncomfortable feelings* tell you that something needs to change. By observing your *comfortable feelings* you will learn a way to recreate these feelings over and over again.

Remember the good feelings!

Many emotions are comfortable. These are the feelings you want to hold on to. Taking good care of yourself will increase them. Such feelings often come quietly. You may not notice them. You may think they won't last.

Do you find yourself thinking—

- "I'm so glad the house is clean . . . but it'll just get messed up again."
- "He says he loves me . . . but can I believe him?"
- "I feel great because the kids are playing together so nicely . . . but it won't last."

Sometimes the unpleasant part of the thought chases away the pleasant part. We forget the comfortable feeling. It doesn't demand as much attention.

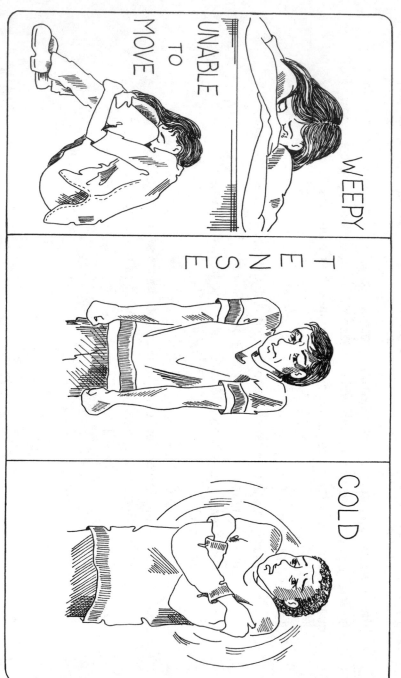

Uncomfortable feelings affect your body unpleasantly.

WEEPY

UNABLE TO MOVE

TENSE

COLD

Some feelings are uncomfortable or even scary. It can be very hard to express these feelings. Sometimes it's almost impossible. Many of us were told not to be angry, or scared, or depressed as children. Even if you are unused to expressing feelings, your body will tell you how you feel. You may feel—

- Hot and sweaty
- Cold and shaky
- Confused
- Tense
- and have an upset stomach or a headache

- Weepy
- Tired or numb
- Unable to move
- Unmotivated

The emotions that produce these changes in your body are strong. Take a moment to remember how your body has felt when you have experienced one of these emotions:

- Fear
- Anger
- Hurt, pain
- Mistrust

- Loneliness
- Jealousy
- Helplessness
- Depression

43

Comfortable feelings affect your body pleasantly.

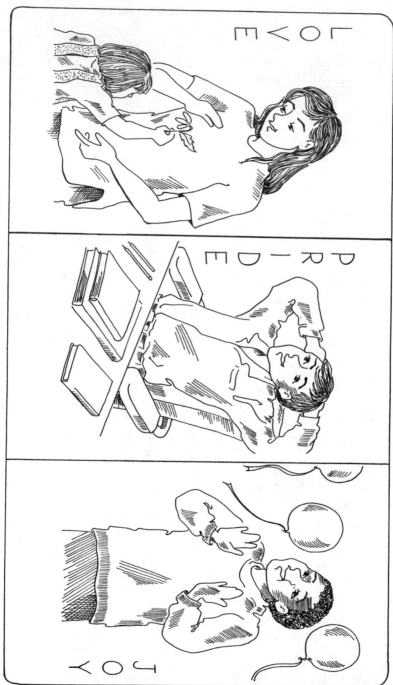

Practice noticing comfortable feelings. Your body will tell you about the comfortable feelings even when you are busy. Notice when you feel—

- Calm
- Relaxed
- Warm or cool
- Light hearted and playful
- Eager
- Rested
- Peaceful
- Loving

Your body reacts pleasantly to—

- Love and affection
- Peace
- Pride
- Hope
- Joy
- Contentment
- Thankfulness
- Confidence
- Recognition
- Support

These are the emotions you want to experience more.

Positive experiences produce positive feelings.

Pay attention to all your feelings. The comfortable feelings and the uncomfortable ones are *both* important. They give you information about yourself. They help you know when you are taking good care of yourself. They also help you realize when you need to change something.

Accept all feelings. It is easy to understand that pleasant feelings are okay. People have a harder time with unpleasant or uncomfortable feelings. They often think they shouldn't have such feelings. But we can't stop ourselves from feeling, anymore than we can stop ourselves from thinking. We can only control how we express our feelings.

Unpleasant feelings are signals that something isn't right. They let you know when you need to change something. They tell you when you need to take better care of yourself.

Anger may cover up other feelings that came first.

Anger, a Powerful Feeling

Anger is a powerful feeling that frightens many people. Anger often covers our feelings of frustration, hurt, or worry. Understanding anger and how you react to it is very important. When people fail to acknowledge their anger, it can control them. If you deny or ignore your anger, you may hurt yourself and others.

Many of us grew up thinking it was wrong to express anger. Our parents may have felt if we expressed anger we were "bad." Some parents confused expressing anger with acts of defiance or aggression. For example, they might have felt that saying, "I hate my sister" was just as bad as knocking her down to the floor and hitting her.

If you don't express the anger you feel in appropriate ways, it will bubble and boil beneath the surface. The anger is bound to explode "inside" or "outside" sooner or later.

Angry outbursts can be reactions to stress.

An "outside" expression of anger may look like a temper tantrum. All the energy comes out in the form of screaming, kicking, hitting, or worse. You may hurt *someone else.*

An "inside" reaction to anger *hurts you.* You may get stomach aches and headaches, or eat too much or not enough. Some people become depressed and can't get anything done. Others drink too much alcohol or take drugs.

Hidden feelings. Anger may not be a response to what is happening right now. Sometimes it is a reaction to a stress. People often get angry when they are having problems with—

- Money
- Housing concerns
- Job
- Relationships
- Poor health
- School
- Housework
- Challenging kids

Many experiences can trigger anger.

Some days just have more stress than we can handle. It is not unusual to be angry because we are scared that we can't cope. However, waiting until you explode when you're angry doesn't take the stress away.

Stress triggers. Many things in life can act as triggers for anger and other stressful feelings. One of the most effective ways to deal with stress is to identify your triggers. They are different for everyone. You've probably noticed how certain things bother your friend, but not you. Maybe she can't stand loud music, but you gain energy from it. Or maybe you like a neat house and your friend happily tolerates a mess.

Triggers can come from our own habits or feelings. At other times triggers are a result of other people's actions or outside events, such as the car breaking down. Triggers are often connected to unmet needs. It is possible to learn to keep triggers from leading to words or actions you might regret later.

How to identify triggers. Triggers often stir up anger or other hurt feelings. Look for the events or activities in your life that cause stress for *you*. Sometimes our own expectations about the way we want things to go can also cause us stress. Once you have identified your triggers, you can move on to learning skills to handle the situations and the feelings they produce.

Examples of triggers that bother some people—

- Deadlines; pressure to get things done
- Not enough time to do things
- Chores that pile up
- Illness or injury
- People who make us uncomfortable
- Embarrassing personal habits
- Feelings of being taken advantage of
- Worry about other people's opinions of us or our kids

✔ ACTIVITY: Identify feelings and triggers that lead to anger

This exercise helps you become aware of the feelings and the triggers in your life that you have *before* you become angry. You can learn how to deal with your feelings *before* they lead to anger. You can learn to recognize your triggers, too.

Write down or tell a friend about a time recently when you felt very angry.

1. Tell about what happened just before you felt angry. Was someone rude to you? Did your child do something you said not to do? Did someone threaten you? Did your child say, "I hate you!"?
2. *Recall how you felt before you became angry: worthless? powerless? scared? unloved?*

When you understand the events and feelings that can lead to anger, you are more able to deal with the situation in a healthy and safe manner.

Before you move on to Part Two, take a deep breath and congratulate yourself. By reading this book, you are taking the time to get to know yourself and your many parts. When you accept yourself as you are, you gain positive "self-esteem." This good feeling gives you the energy to try new things and to make changes.

Self-understanding is an important tool for creating positive change in your life. You can now recognize what you need to take care of yourself and your children. You can now notice more quickly the feelings and situations which get in your way. By understanding who you are and what you need, you can begin to set goals to grow in new ways.

Part Two

Skills and Tools that Help Me Take Care of Myself (and My Children)

You can improve your life by changing some things.

JOEY, WHY CAN'T YOU GET ALONG AT SCHOOL! YOU'RE NOT DOING WHAT YOU ARE TOLD TO DO! I'M ASHAMED !!

STEP #1: MEET WITH JOEY'S TEACHER

I THINK IF WE ALL WORK TOGETHER JOEY CAN IMPROVE . . .

I DON'T LIKE SCHOOL ANYWAY!

STEP #2: HELP IN THE CLASSROOM ONCE A WEEK

YOU'RE DOING GREAT WORK, SALLY.

I NEED TO STOP NAGGING. IT DIDN'T HELP WHEN MY MOTHER NAGGED AT ME. I NEED TO GET INVOLVED IN JOEY'S EDUCATION...

STEP #3: USE ENCOURAGEMENT

JOEY, I'M VERY PROUD OF YOUR EFFORT!

I LIKE MY TEACHER!

Think about Change

When you know yourself well, you may begin to notice things you would like to change. You can't change your temperament, or what happened in the past. You can do things differently now, however. Look at the decisions you have *already* made that helped you grow and feel good.

The more helpful decisions you make, the more self-confident you feel. This self-confidence helps you be a more effective parent.

As a parent, some of the things you may need are:
- Energy to get things done
- Time for yourself and your children
- Information to help make good decisions
- Healthy ways to deal with stress
- Problem-solving skills

It is easy to blame others for problems.

Obstacles to change. Daily stresses can make it hard to think change is possible. Some of these stresses are—

- Partners or children who need or demand more than we can give
- Fatigue and frustration
- Lack of enough money for basic needs
- Illness that prevents us from doing what we need to do

Blaming others. Frustration can lead us to blame others for our circumstances. It's easy to say, "I can't get anything done because the kids are bothering me." Or, "I can't help the way I am. My parents got divorced when I was little." Or, "The landlord is really mean, so now I don't have a place to live."

Blaming others is a tempting way to deal with the stresses in life. It takes the burden from your shoulders and puts it somewhere else. However, you can only change when you take responsibility. A better way to take care of stress is to change your point of view.

Recognize problem areas and resolve to make changes.

Steps to change. Four things are necessary when making changes in your life. They are—

- Acceptance

    Accept who you are now.

    Accept that you can't control all influences in your life.

    Recognize that you do have the power to grow and change.

- Choice

    Choose to do things in new ways.

    Stop making excuses or blaming others.

- Commitment

    Set reachable goals. Start with something easy.

    Stick with your goals long enough to reach them.

    Congratulate yourself at every gain, no matter how small it seems.

- Responsibility

    Say, "This is my life. I'm in charge of it."

    Accept mistakes and go on.

    Feel good that you can take responsibility for your own actions.

These ways help you think about change.

ALONE

SOME OF MY BEST MEMORIES ARE OF FISHING WITH MY DAD. IT'S GOOD TO SPEND SOME QUIET TIME TO THINK.

WITH A FRIEND

I FOUND MYSELF YELLING AT THE KIDS ALL DAY. I COULDN'T SEEM TO STOP MYSELF. I FEEL MUCH BETTER SINCE I'VE SPENT THIS ½ HOUR WITH YOU, CAROL.

ON PAPER

TODAY, I NOTICED THAT I WAS VERY NERVOUS. I COULDN'T GET ANYTHING DONE.

✔ ACTIVITY: What do I want to change in my life?

Think about a day in your life. Share with a friend how you felt. Or write about your day. Take time to get everything down on paper. When you make the effort to express your thoughts, you learn much more about yourself. You will discover *what* you want to change.

Here are some questions to help you get started—

- What happened during the day?
- Describe the feelings you had throughout the day.
- What did you do? Did you make helpful decisions?
- What did you need? Did you or someone else meet the needs?
- What did you like or dislike about the day's activities or emotions?
- What would you change about that day if you could go back and re-do it?

You can learn tools to deal with stresses.

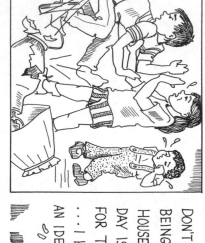

Deal with Feelings and Needs

When we express strong feelings in unhealthy ways, we hurt ourselves and others. There are three effective tools for changing the way we express feelings. If you practice these tools often, in time they may become automatic. They can help you in your relationships with family, friends, and co-workers.

Time-out is a tool that helps calm body and emotions. It allows you to get away from the stressful situation. It gives you time to think and relax.

Redirection allows you to replace negative thoughts with positive ones. You can change your view of a situation or a person with this tool.

Prevention is a tool to take care of your needs and your responsibilities in ways that prevent conflicts and over-reaction.

Time-out helps you calm down before you take action.

✔ **ACTIVITY: Before feelings reach the boiling point, take a *time-out.*** Here are three things to do when you need to calm down. Doing these things can help you be in control of your feelings, words, and actions. Time-out gives you extra energy to handle a stressful situation.

1. *Find a quiet spot.* This can be outside or in another area away from the stress. Go there before things begin to get out of control. Take a few minutes, or as long as necessary, to calm down.
2. *Breathe deeply.* As you breathe in, count slowly to five. As you breathe out, count to five again. Close your eyes. Imagine a quite, enjoyable place.
3. *Relax the muscles in your body.* Lie down if possible, or sit comfortably. Start with your feet. As you breathe in, tighten your feet. Then as you breathe out, relax the muscles. Notice the warm energy move to your feet. Continue this process up through your legs and the rest of your body.

Redirection helps you solve problems peacefully.

Redirection. Sometimes when we feel upset we have a great deal of energy. To use that energy we need to *redirect* it toward healthy thoughts and actions. Redirection means to—

- Focus on ways to make things better
- Change unpleasant thoughts or actions
- Begin to solve the problem

Use these four phrases to redirect your reaction to a person or situation:

1. "*I feel* . . . irritated by the kids' noise and roughhousing."
2. "*I need* . . . peace and quiet to get this work done."
3. "*The kids need* . . . to play because they are full of energy."
4. "*I can* . . . ask them to play outside or I can play with them for a while, and work later when they have gone to bed."

Redirect your energy toward healthy action.

WHAT'S THE MATTER WITH EVERYONE!! WHY ARE YOU SO NOISY! CAN'T YOU KIDS PLAY QUIETLY?

HERE I GO AGAIN!... I AM PACING... AND NAGGING AT THE KIDS TOO MUCH!!

HEY! THEY'RE JUST PLAYING. I'M THE ONE WHO NEEDS A "TIME OUT!"

WHAT I REALLY NEED RIGHT NOW IS TO FEEL LIKE I'M DOING SOMETHING USEFUL WITH MY ENERGY....

I KNOW! I LIKE FLOWERS. I HAVE A PLANTER AND I CAN MAKE THE TIME...

✔ ACTIVITY: Redirect your energy in positive ways.

- *Lie on the floor with your feet up and place a cool cloth over your face.* Focus on a calming word, thought, or picture. Do this for five minutes.
- *Notice what negative thoughts are racing through your head.* Replace every "if," "but," "should," and "can't" with the image of a balloon. Pop the balloon or let it float away from you. Let the negative thoughts go.
- *Do something physical.* Walk, ride a bike, swim, rake the yard, brush the dog, wash the car, etc. Avoid sharp, heavy movements. Use long, even movements that are relaxing.
- *Write down your thoughts and feelings.* List the things you like to do. Get the unpleasant thoughts out of your head and onto paper.
- *Talk with a friend.* Sometimes friends can help us see things in new ways. It helps if the friend feels he or she can be honest with you.

You can prevent problems from occurring.

Prevention. As you begin to recognize and deal with feelings, you will learn to prevent problems from occuring. Three important steps to prevention are—

1. Plan routines that help you meet your needs. For example, get up early so that you have time to get yourself ready before you have to get the kids up.
2. Practice the routines you choose until they become habits.
3. Take responsibility for your feelings. Noticing your feelings helps you deal with each situation. When you meet your needs, you have energy to take care of yourself and your children.

Plan ahead to prevent stress before it occurs.

Planning ahead can help prevent stress. When you think ahead you can plan for the day's events. You can also plan new ways to react to situations which often trigger frustration or anger.

Try this planning process the next time you feel frustrated or overwhelmed—

1. "*I feel* . . . frustrated at dinnertime."
2. "*I need* . . . to fix dinner without hassles from anybody."
3. "*The kids need* . . . instant food and more time to play."
4. "*I can* . . . give them a healthy snack. I can let them know when dinner is nearly ready."

Plan ways to prevent day-to-day problems in your family.

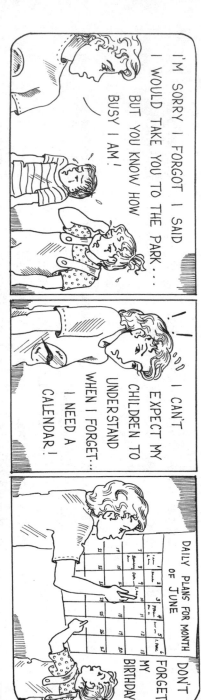

Here are some other ways planning ahead can help you focus on what's important so that life flows more smoothly.

Keep a calendar in the kitchen on which you write all appointments and activities for your family. Teach everyone who is old enough to refer to it. This can relieve angry feelings over forgotten appointments. You can also notice if you are trying to do too much for others and not enough for yourself.

Make a chart with words and pictures of the things your child needs to do, like getting ready for day care or school. Put it on the refrigerator where the child can see it easily. She can look at it to remind herself. You will be happier because you aren't nagging her. She will be learning how to be independent.

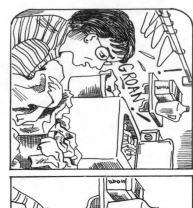

Plan time and money to spend on yourself, too.

A chart of the hours in a day or week allows you to write in when you have to work and when your children will need you the most. It is also important to reserve time for yourself when you make up the chart. The hardest thing for parents is getting enough time alone for rest and recreation. Mark your time on the chart. Then it will be easier for you to say, "This half hour is for me."

A budget helps you plan how to make ends meet. Think of it as a picture that shows how much money you have and what you are doing with it. If you don't like how the picture looks, you can make changes. Using resources (time, money, things, energy) wisely relieves a great deal of stress. You can buy a budget workbook in a bookstore or variety store that shows you how to make a budget; it also gives you room to write down your monthly income and spending.

Create time to take care of your physical needs.

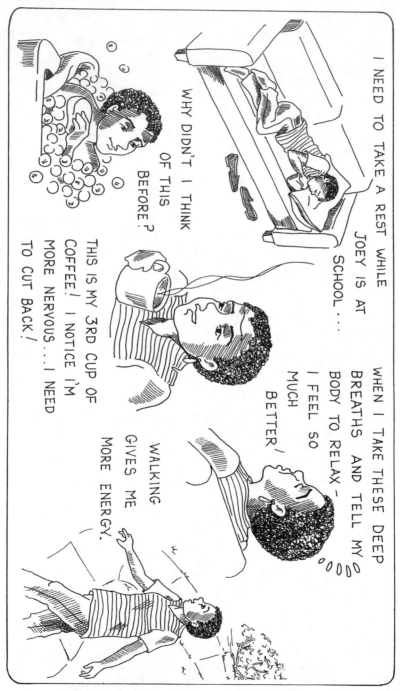

I NEED TO TAKE A REST WHILE JOEY IS AT SCHOOL...

WHEN I TAKE THESE DEEP BREATHS AND TELL MY BODY TO RELAX - I FEEL SO MUCH BETTER!

WHY DIDN'T I THINK OF THIS BEFORE?

WALKING GIVES ME MORE ENERGY.

THIS IS MY 3RD CUP OF COFFEE! I NOTICE I'M MORE NERVOUS...I NEED TO CUT BACK!

Take care of your physical health so that you have energy to cope with stresses. Prevent health-related stresses, such as getting too tired or hurt. Simple activities and changes in routine can give you more energy, also.

- Make reasonable plans for how much you can do in a day. Slow down.
- Plan to do the hardest activities when you have the most energy.
- Improve eating habits. Quit eating anything that makes you feel bad.
- Get enough sleep and exercise to improve your energy level.
- Stop activities that hurt your body (drinking, drugs, smoking, etc.).
- Get medical help when you need it.
- Do activities that are fun and relaxing for you.

Communication means both talking and listening.

MAMÁ, THANK YOU FOR
LISTENING TO HOW I
FEEL. I AM REALLY
TRYING TO DO
BETTER!

MARIA, I AM PROUD
OF YOU. YOU AND
I REALLY LISTENED
TO EACH OTHER.
WE WERE ABLE
TO SOLVE THE
PROBLEM.
IT IS IMPORTANT
TO UNDERSTAND
HOW WE FEEL.
I LOVE YOU!

How to Listen, How to Talk

Effective communication helps us take care of ourselves better. With effective listening and talking, many issues never become problems. When there is a problem, effective talking and listening can help solve it.

Communication means listening to the feelings and needs of other people. It means saying clearly what you feel and need. Good communication leads to understanding. Understanding and being understood help people work together to get things done.

Two tools help people communicate better to solve problems. They are—
- I-statements
- Active listening

Communicate your feelings with "I-statements."

I-statements. I-statements tell others how you feel and what you need. They give people a chance to understand you. To use I-statements—

1. *Begin with your feelings*: "I feel . . . worried and angry . . ."
2. *Describe the situation* that is bothering you. Continue, " . . . when you don't come home on time."
3. *Say what you need* to solve the problem. "I need . . . you to be on time, or to call me if you're going to be late."

Such clear statements allow you to express the problem simply. Step number 3 may allow for negotiation. You have, however, been clear about what you need. You and the other person can arrive at a solution more easily.

Show that you heard by using "active listening."

Active listening. Active listening helps you hear and accept the feelings of others. It is more than hearing the words. You want to hear the *feelings*, too. Most of what we say is not in words. It is in body language and tone of voice. Words only tell you part of what a person is saying. When you use active listening—

1. Listen to words: "I'm not hungry."

2. Say what you think the other person is feeling: "I bet you feel resentful about stopping your fun right now."

3. Describe what you see happening: "You'd rather keep playing with your friend than come in for dinner."

4. Ask the person what he or she needs: "Do you need a little more time to play? Would you like me to call you in 5 or 10 minutes?"

Solve problems with I-statements and active listening.

JOSE, REMEMBER TO PUT YOUR NEW BIKE AWAY BEFORE YOU COME IN.

OK, MOM —

BUT, MOM! IT'S SO HARD FOR ME TO REMEMBER TO DO IT!

ACTIVE LISTENING

YOU ARE TELLING ME THAT YOU HAVE TROUBLE PUTTING THE BIKE AWAY. WHAT WILL HELP YOU TO REMEMBER?

LATER

I'M HOME

I-STATEMENT

JOSE, I AM CONCERNED ABOUT YOUR BIKE! IT IS NOT PUT AWAY!

OOPS!

BRAINSTORMING A CONSEQUENCE

OK, MOM, I'LL REMEMBER TO PUT MY BIKE AWAY. IF I DON'T DO IT, I AGREE NOT TO RIDE IT FOR A DAY ... THANKS!

You can solve most problems more easily by using the tools of I-statements and active listening. When there are problems, each person involved has feelings and needs. It is important to find solutions that meet everyone's needs. This is part of taking care of yourself and others.

When solving a problem, it helps if everyone uses I-statements and active listening. Your children will learn how to use them if you teach them. Model the process for them. Practice it until it becomes a habit for you and for your children.

Work together with your child to solve problems.

MAMA, MAMA! YOU NEVER LISTEN TO ME!

I NEED TO HANG UP! I CAN'T HEAR YOU!

THE PROBLEM:

LET'S THINK OF WAYS TO WORK THIS OUT FOR BOTH OF US.

LOOK FOR IDEAS:

YOU ARE TELLING ME THAT YOU FEEL LEFT OUT WHEN I AM BUSY TALKING ON THE PHONE . . .

GATHER INFORMATION:

I WILL AGREE TO STOP TALKING ON THE PHONE AFTER 10 MINUTES. WE CAN SET THE TIMER WHILE YOU WAIT . . . AND YOU AGREE NOT TO INTERRUPT ME.

MAKE YOUR DECISION AND . . .

BUT, WHEN I AM ON THE PHONE I NEED TO BE ABLE TO HEAR MY FRIEND.

DECIDE WHAT YOU WANT:

WHEN I AM DONE, YOU WILL HAVE MY ATTENTION. IS THAT OKAY?

OKAY—

FOLLOW THROUGH

Five steps to solving problems

Use I-statements and active listening when you follow these five steps to solve problems effectively.

1. *Describe the problem.* Be specific about the action or words which bother you.
2. *Gather information.* When does it happen? Why?
3. *Decide what you want.* What do you want instead?
4. *Look for ideas.* Brainstorm as many ideas as possible. The more ideas you have, the more likely you are to find several that will work.
5. *Make your decision and follow through.* Change to a different idea if the one you chose didn't work. Change as often as you need to until you find something that works to solve the problem.

Begin with one area you would like to work on.

Support Change

The tools and skills in this book will help you to solve problems. Change does not happen quickly. It's hard to know what to do all the time. It's hard to have reasonable expectations. It's easy to feel discouraged.

To make changes that will last, you will want to set reasonable goals. Start with one area you would like to change. For example, you might decide to—

- Make plans (think ahead) to finish a project
- Spend half an hour a day reading to or playing games with your children
- Practice using I-statements and active listening when the kids bug you
- Work on one of your triggers (page 53)

Decide what behavior you want to work on.

✔ ACTIVITY: Set goals in order to do something important.

Set goals. Decide the area you want to work on. Follow these steps to set your goal. See pages 35-36 also for a review of the goal-setting process.

1. *Choose a reasonable goal* that you can accomplish in a short time. After you practice and succeed with small goals, long-term goals will be easier.

2. *Decide the steps to take* to reach the goal. For example, you might decide to find childcare for two weeks while you look for a job. Write down the steps to take in getting childcare.

3. *Decide when you will start.* How long do you think it will take to reach your goal? Setting a time limit will help you work more effectively toward the goal.

4. *Congratulate yourself* when you reach the goal.

When you set a goal and reach it, it is easier to do it again. Decide another area to work on and set another goal.

Encourage yourself to try new things.

Encouragement. Encourage yourself and your children. Remember that everyone makes mistakes. You continue to love your children when they make mistakes. Continue to love yourself, too. Change takes time and is not always easy. Practice encouragement by doing the following:

- Plan your days to avoid triggers that stress you.
- Notice what you (or partner or children) do well. Write down at least one good thing about every day. Then post this on the refrigerator where everyone can see it.
- Notice your efforts to make effective changes, even if the result you want isn't there yet. Remember that change takes time. Compliment yourself for continuing to try.
- Decide what to do differently next time when you make a mistake. A mistake is not a failure. A mistake is a chance to learn.
- When you feel discouraged, try something small. Focus on what you can do.
- Take time to have fun. Laugh and play each day.

Encourage yourself with affirmations.

Affirmations. Encouraging statements about yourself or others are called affirmations. The idea of an affirmation is to replace negative thoughts about yourself or others with positive ones. It takes practice. It may also feel awkward at first if you are not accustomed to accepting compliments.

If you give yourself compliments often enough, you will begin to believe them. When you feel good about yourself, it shows in what you do and say. Practice affirmations like these, or others you think up—

- "I am proud of myself. I tried something new."
- "I am a loving parent. The kids and I had a good day."
- "I know I can do this. I'll be patient with myself."
- "I solved that problem!"
- "I exercised five days out of seven this week. Hooray for me!"

Unpleasant thoughts wear you down.

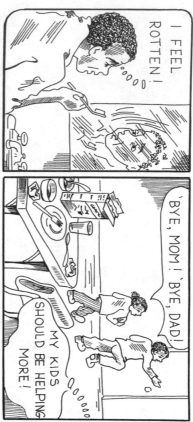

Unpleasant thoughts can wear us down in no time. They can be about ourselves or about other people. These thoughts can affect how we feel and behave. When you notice you are having lots of negative thoughts—STOP! Try to think of a positive thing to say about yourself or others.

Give *affirmations* as often as possible. Remember that your children will follow your example. You might say—

- "You give nice hugs."
- "That was a terrific idea you had."
- "I enjoyed being with you today."
- "We accomplished a lot together."
- "I'm so glad you are my son/daughter."

Look for support from the people around you.

Get support. People were not meant to live alone in the world. It takes help and support from others to get through life. We get more out of our lives when we both accept and offer help. Build as many caring relationships as you can. Here are some things you might do.

- Spend time getting to know relatives, friends, and neighbors. You can help them and they can help you.
- Get to know the parents of your children's friends. You can support each other.
- Invite friends over for snacks, games, and conversation. The children can play together while the adults visit.
- Call someone in your class or support group to "check in" once a week. Talk about what you're learning.
- Find someone at your job whom you would like to get to know. Invite her or him to share the lunch hour with you.

Businesses and services in your community offer help.

Community resources. Look for these sources of help and encouragement in your neighborhood.

- Schools. Learn about your child's educational and social needs and abilities. Join the PTA.
- Churches, synagogues, and other places of worship. Make friends. Nurture your spirit.
- Public health offices and hospitals. Get medical care, health information, and classes.
- Mental health agencies. Obtain counseling, attend support groups and classes.
- Social service agencies. Get help with family support, housing, medical needs, child care, and financial aid.
- Schools for adults. Attend job skills classes, GED and high school classes, community college and college classes.
- Counselors. Obtain help with personal and family problems.
- Libraries. Enjoy children's activities, movies, books, classes, information.

Congratulations! We wish you health and happiness.

Congratulations and Best Wishes!

Taking care of yourself takes time and effort. You've worked hard reading this book and learning the tools it offers. What you are doing for yourself will help your family, too.

Self-esteem grows as you accept your feelings, needs, limitations, and abilities. It grows when you make positive changes in your life. Changes for the better help you take control of your life.

You are responsible for how you respond to your life, even when you can't control all events or other people. You've learned a lot about how to take care of yourself. Practice what you've learned until it all becomes habit. Your children will learn from your positive example.

You are now able to give your children the best you have to offer: *YOU!*

Index

Bold numbers indicate activity pages.

Order these books for quick ideas

Tools for Everyday Parenting Series

Illustrated. Paperback, $11.95 each; library binding, $18.95 each

These books are geared for new or frustrated parents. Fun to look at and fun to read, they present information in both words and cartoons. They are perfect for parents who may be busy with school, jobs, or other responsibilities and who have little time to read.

Magic Tools for Raising Kids, by Elizabeth Crary • Parenting young children is easier and more effective with a toolbox of useful, child-tested, positive tools. Learn what to do, how to do it, and what to say to make raising lovable, self-confident kids easier.
128 pages, ISBN 0-943990-77-7 paperback, 0-943990-78-5 library

365 Wacky, Wonderful Ways to Get Your Children to Do What You Want, by Elizabeth Crary • Young children share certain behaviors that are calculated to drive parents crazy. Here are hundreds of practical (and sometimes zany) ideas to help parents cope.
104 pages, ISBN 0-943990-79-3 paperback, 0-943990-80-7 library

More books and ordering information on next page

Order these books for quick ideas

More books on preceding page. Paperback, $11.95 each; library binding, $18.95 each

Peekaboo and Other Games to Play with Your Baby, by Shari Steelsmith • Babies love games and this book is full of games they enjoy at different stages of development. All games help develop skills, are fun, and strengthen the bond between baby and parent.
120 pages, ISBN 0-943990-81-5 paperback, 0-943990-99-8 library

Joyful Play with Toddlers: Recipes for Fun with Odds and Ends, by Sandi Dexter • Toddlers at play are full of curiosity and daring. They need creative and safe ways to express themselves. Parents need lots of ideas for no-cost or low-cost toys, games, and activities.
128 pages, ISBN 1-884734-00-6 paperback, 1-884734-01-4 library

Taking Care of Me (So I Can Take Care of My Children), by Barbara Carlson, Margaret Healy, Glo Wellman • By taking care of themselves, parents can take care of their children (and others) better. Learn how temperament, childhood experiences, basic needs, and goals affect parenting style.
112 pages, ISBN 1-884734-02-2 paperback, 1-884734-03-0 library

Ask for these books at your favorite bookstore, or call toll free 1-800-992-6657. VISA and MasterCard accepted with phone orders. Complete book catalog available on request.

Parenting Press, Inc., Dept. 701, P.O. Box 75267, Seattle, WA 98175
www.ParentingPress.com
In Canada, call **Raincoast Books Distribution Co.,** 1-800-663-5714.
Prices subject to change without notice.